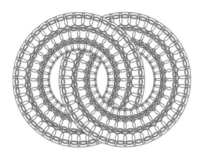

The Curve of Things

The Curve of Things

Kathy Kremins

Foreword by Ysabel Y. Gonzalez

CAVANKERRY PRESS

CavanKerry Press Ltd.
Fort Lee, New Jersey
www.cavankerrypress.org

Publisher's Cataloging-in-Publication Data
provided by Five Rainbows Cataloging Services
Names: Kremins, Kathy, author. | Gonzalez, Ysabel Y., writer of foreword.
Title: The curve of things / Kathy Kremins ; foreword by Ysabel Y. Gonzalez.
Description: Fort Lee, NJ : CavanKerry Press, 2024.
Identifiers: ISBN 978-1-960327-05-5 (paperback)
Subjects: LCSH: Poetry—Women authors. | Queer poetry. | Intersectionality
    (Sociology)—Poetry. | Immigrants—Poetry. | American poetry. | Irish
    poetry. | BISAC: POETRY / LGBTQ+. | POETRY / Women Authors.
Classification: LCC PN6109.9 .K74 2024 (print) | DDC 811/.6—dc23.

Cover Artwork: "Rewind" by Sarah Klein. https://skleinstudio.com/
Cover and interior text design by Mayfly Design
First Edition 2024, Printed in the United States of America

CavanKerry Press is proud to present the fifth book in the Florenz Eisman Memorial Series—fine collections by New Jersey poets, notable or emerging. A gifted poet and great lover of poetry herself, Florenz was the publisher's partner in establishing the press and CavanKerry's Managing Editor from its inception in 2000 until her passing in 2013. Her ideas and intelligence were a great source of inspiration for writers and staff alike as were her quick wit and signature red lipstick.

Made possible by funds from the New Jersey State Council on the Arts, a partner agency of the National Endowment for the Arts.

CavanKerry Press is grateful for the generous support it receives from the New Jersey State Council on the Arts, as well as the following funders:

The Academy of American Poets

Community of Literary Magazines and Presses

National Book Foundation

New Jersey Arts and Culture Renewal Fund

New Jersey Economic Development Authority

The Poetry Foundation

Also by Kathy Kremins

An Ethics of Reading: The Broken Beauties of Toni Morrison,
  Nawal El Saadawi, and Arundhati Roy (2010)

Undressing the World (2022)

Seamus & His Smalls (2023)

FOR YOU, DEAR ONE

Will I cherish you, adore you, make way for you,
make myself better for you, look at you
and always see you, tell you the truth?
And if love is not those things then what things?

—Jeanette Winterson,
Written on the Body

Contents

Foreword

When Kathy and I found each other, we were in the midst
of quarantining during a pandemic. A few of us formed a
women's collective while afraid and aching, trying to find
connection in any ways that would fill us and help us stay
empowered. Since then, we have found each other's shine in
the ache—going on writing retreats together, breaking bread,
sharing each other's worlds over the phone. And then, there
is our shared love language: poetry. We constantly exchange
notes on what we're reading and what is feeding us. Kathy
strongly advocates for us to study her influences like Audre
Lorde, Adrienne Rich, June Jordan, Cheryl Clarke. We are
constantly discussing how we can live radicalism and support
repair in the BIPOC, LGBTQIA, and differently abled
communities. I have deep gratitude in witnessing Kathy's
poems from *The Curve of Things* manifest themselves and grow
from seeds into fruit.

Kathy and I are not women who write in silos, so
community is at the core of our initiatives—to be better
human beings and advocate for vulnerable communities.
Communities we belong to, communities we thrive in. Leaving
the world a much more tender place is where our work
intersects and where I continue to learn from my dear friend.
This gift of women like Kathy in my life has been one of the
greatest blessings I've ever discovered: to be in community with
such women whose poems hold the same values as mine—
justice, vulnerability, compassion, and love. Always love.

And how does love feel in your hands, dear reader? Sticky and sweet? Fluid and dripping through cupped hands? Does it laugh with you or hold an orange in its palm? When reading *The Curve of Things*, I asked myself not only how love feels, but what draws me to it, what it tastes like, and whether it makes my body quiver. When I first read *The Curve of Things*, I said "my body does that too!" In the loving, the grieving, holding space for the ones we adore—how I've ached, rejoiced. But also felt the hard edges where love isn't quite circular or smooth but in fact messy. Still love, nonetheless. The more complicated, the more resilient we become because of it.

Kathy Kremins maps a nonlinear journey, circular and round, on loving women. From "Coming Out in Dublin, 1980" she writes,

> And these women in their curious attentiveness
>
> expect me, an American with a mind and body
> but without a soul to radiate
> the sex of language

and throughout this collection Kathy truly does "radiate / the sex of language" with intimate, sometimes painfully tender moments. She gives herself permission to grieve while loving, providing her readers with spaciousness, allowing us to carry the weight of grief alongside her. This book is a door to permissions, so we do more than just grieve alongside her— we resist, squirm, rise, fall, and eat with her. And this book is also a lesson on how to love the author. She opens with the poem "Diversity of Matter" and states, "I'll show you where to touch me," pointedly asking us, her dear community of family, friends, and readers, to engage in intimacy alongside her. If you are brave, this author will take you on this journey of loving and loss that teaches me that we must be brave in the writing of vulnerabilities, as well have tenderness in the reading of soft and courageous moments.

Not all storms destroy.
Most rearrange the landscape
in a way imperceptible to the eye,
but the tree knows, adjusts,
and becomes steadier.

In these poems, Kathy helps me to connect to the messy aspects of humanity and helps me to not dismiss these parts so quickly but sit with them and meditate on the brokenness and how that, too, can feed us, support our very own transformation if we so choose it. Kathy helps me to also be more tender with myself in order to forgive myself and learn how to gently tend to my body—become "steadier."

As a culture bearer, activist, advocate, vital member of the New Jersey community, Kathy Kremins is a crucial voice that bellows from the queer community and beyond. Her stories and poems reaffirm that love, in any language or identity, will save us all. Bearing witness to love and all its flaws, and even admitting the loneliness of it, takes a deep talent, which you will witness in the pages of this collection. Who, if not a poet, can help humanity see the truth most clearly—on loving and leaving—in order for us to be our most authentic and best selves? This poet certainly has done so for me.

Ysabel Y. Gonzalez,
author of *Wild Invocations*
Washington, New Jersey
June 2023

Diversity of Matter

Before there was a periodic table,
there was chaos.
Some call me unruly,
but life is an experiment,
a search for patterns,
deriving relationships and
predicting behaviors.
It's a chemical thing.

chlorine bromine iodine
calcium strontium barium
sulfur selenium tellurium

Breaking the law is the law.

law of triads
telluric screw
law of octaves

I'll show you where to touch me.

1

angles of discovery

The Curve of Things

Loving a woman is not linear;
it is filled with half-moons, semicircles,
partial eclipses of the sun,
two halves rolling
into new geometric configurations,
sensuous and infinite.

China cups, cereal bowls,
a sunflower's center, your lips on my lips,
a puppy's head, your lower back,
the mountain's outline, the stars at night,
a new moon, an old wooden barrel,
your hands cupped, filled with water,
the yellowed pear, the brass doorknob,
the city's skyline in my rearview mirror,
the brush in my hand, the sleeping cat,
the printed letter G, a slow word,
your breasts in profile, my mouth on your neck,
the silt-rich molehills, a scared possum,
the crystal goblet half-filled, a globe,
an enjambed line, a lullaby,
a baby's pout, the geography of your foot.

Halos of cigar smoke, newly permed hair,
dabs of frost on windows, the tips of your fingers,
a cold beer bottle, a hot cup of coffee,
a beagle's howl, the rabbit's route,
my breath on your cheek, red, juicy tomatoes,
the binding of a book, the tension in the bowstrings,
a kind word, a quick pivot,
the physics of baseball, the swelling in a joint,
the brown cowl of the Franciscan, a tattooed bicep,
the topography of your inner thigh, a half-bitten peach,

an alto sax, a comb through your hair,
a backward dive, a pebble,
waves before they crash, the final burst of sunset,
a mother and child rocking, painting a female nude,
a back arching in ecstasy, a cat before pouncing,
a movie screen, your soft moans.

The dog chasing his tail, an embryo floating,
the moon rises full, a nova bursts forth,
a belly protrudes, a knapsack explodes,
your closed lids flutter, ice freezes into cubes,
a signature is written, bristles stroke a canvas,
a scar under your chin, Brancusi's birds,
a cliff at sunrise, milk on an upper lip,
your eyes in moonlight, the silky lampshade,
the sculptor's knife, your half-closed lips,
a recently emptied seat, cinnamon sweet potatoes,
a ballerina's calf, a used bar of soap,
Chubby Checker's "The Twist," your head in my lap,
reading a favorite poem, the chiming of our nose rings,
a braid of gold on a finger, a bowl of chocolate pudding,
your tongue on my nipple, my hands memorizing your body.

Loving a woman
lies in the curve of things.

Chocolate

Another December, gray and cold.
Month of holidays, shopping, families,
and I walk alone in the streets of my memories
to that house on 4th Street with Patches barking

as I open the door to Gary
giving me a high five and grabbing my hand,
my first time walking with a boy that way.
We go to the corner, past the big boys,

teenagers, and into the candy store
that is more newspapers and magazines,
cigarettes and stale coffee than candy.
You hold my hand, watch me as if I am

a precious shiny stone—
and I know you are poor too,
but on my tippy toes, I reach the top shelf.
You never let go

never change that ever-sweet smile,
dig into your pocket,
and place the dime on the counter.
We leave without anything for you,

but your happiness never wavers.
Past those hooligans, yelling shit,
you never blink

until we pause for me to unwrap
that piece of chocolate, the way years later
I undress a lover who leaves only bruises,
while you unpeel a radiant orange

pulled from your jacket
as if making a fire in your hands,
and I am sad to say that a boy will never
make me feel so safe and warm again.

Coming Out in Dublin, 1980

Rose parades me to the bar like a prize,
a wild American with her first passport
and appetite for the angles of discovery,

huddling at a dusty corner table on wobbly chairs
to meet Irish women at Ryan's Pub where,
most nights and afternoons, a sparse clump of men

grayed in their sameness spit anger at their lives,
leave wages on the counter,
go home to rage some more.

On Sunday nights at Ryan's Pub
queer women struggle to utter
words that resemble love

like so much else unsaid in Ireland.
There is distance here—
as if desire hasn't been born yet.

Clinks of glass on wood and
suspended hum of female inflection,
tables are full

but weight is lacking.
No music and no dancing,
faces framed in a halo of dirt

painted on a pale wall,
posed in their doubt.
And these women in their curious attentiveness

expect me, an American with a mind and body
but without a soul, to radiate
the sex of language

so they might connect
beyond the bitter beer, sticky tables, and
cold dampness of a cellar bar

in the shadow of St. Colum's Church,
so that someday they might dance away from shame
to the turning of a naked woman

Celtic cross tattooed on her breast,
skin dusted with smoky peat,
sweet grass, and crackling air.

The Fall

The cranberries soft
as a hammock, we sway,
held spellbound, mesmerized
by the curve of your fingers
in the red, dripping juice,
write love letters.
Moisture between my breasts,
seeping inward,
your crescent thighs
a ruse to entice me
into such a cloistered garden,
and I have fallen
harder than Eve.

Blowing Kisses

One of those stories told too many times
of how my father almost died from a burst heart
and I, only four, oblivious to the possible grief,
wave to my father, looking from the hospital window
at his little girl offered up in my mother's arms,
blowing kisses in a direction lined with absence.

While you stand on the train platform, sad, anticipating,
once again, our separation in life's labyrinth,
my fingers are guided to my lips by an unseen hand
and I blow gently the kisses, grasping the memory of the body,
thinking I hear my father hum a little tune
as the tears fall into another temporary loss.

Wild West

As if a Jersey girl in Utah wasn't wild enough
said girl kissing her first girlfriend, first love

on the edge of Inspiration Point, crimson
hoodoos rising spire-like across

Bryce Canyon at sunset, days later
balanced at sunrise at Sunrise Point

stretched into space looking for the best angle
leaning over the jagged crags to catch a photo

shot after red-rising shot, rapid-fire as I totter
slip, trip—now in my slow-motion memory—

reach back with my left hand toward earth
the Nikon from my right hand tumbles

into the abyss of the gorge. I still feel your fingers
dig into my shoulder, pulling me back from uncertain death,

the blast of the crashing camera echoing like my bones—
certainly not the last time you saved me from me.

About the Sadness

I just wanted to know about the sadness
That propelled you
Around campus. Your long black hair,
Face so pained I was drawn to it.
Was it my kindness, or curiosity?
In the dorm during that snowstorm,
I passed you, stranded
In the phone booth and knew you were desperate,
Slumped in the dark corner
In the cellar of an ancient building.
I thought you might be crying.

I thought you might be crying
So I spoke to you.
Years later (when all of you were so engrained
In my eyes and hands and mouth and tongue)
You let me into that phone booth
And the child you aborted
For your boyfriend who wasn't ready.
What about you pulling my head
To your breast and begging me to suck?

To your breast and begging me to suck,
I was already deeper into you
Than I could have known,
Loving you with my mouth
Safe for you and coming
As my tongue replaced the dick,
Arching backward
Pulling my hair, wanting me deeper,
Crying many nights, apologizing
For ruining my life.

I didn't understand you then.
I understand even less now.

I understand even less now
How you wanted me to hold you at night
(Or at least the nights you needed my touch),
While on other nights I fucked you
Opening your legs wide and you begged
For me to rip out your womb.
All I could do was brush your hair
With my lips and remember
How you once wanted me
Like the end of the world, and you were about to come.

Like the end of the world and you were about to come
Underneath this young guy you met
At the bar, my cousin's friend,
And I pretend to sleep
With my back to the sex
As he grunts and groans, but you're quiet
Not like the woman who moans
And calls my name as my fingers
Move to the slow wave of your hips,
Licking the red nipples
With quick flicks of my tongue
Knowing what you like better
I come without you ever touching me.

I come without you ever touching me.
I stay with you in the waiting room.
Three months pregnant for the second time,
I sit with you wanting that baby
For us. It is not mine
And it won't be yours as you disappear

Into that clinic room
That will wipe away memory and replace
It with an anguish you hide daily.
In recovery, I hold your hand.
You don't hold back, unburdened
Of the little love you had left.

Of the little love you had left
You buried your body close to me
For comfort I longed to give you
Already past the time
When either of us could feel.
Later I found you crumpled over the toilet
Crying for the embryo lost in the blood,
The baby they failed to take in the botched
Abortion, the child I flushed.
You crawled into my lap
On that cold bathroom floor
To say goodbye in heaving sobs, pleading
For me to always love you, frightened
I just wanted to know about the sadness.

A Vespers of Sorts

The asymmetrical plot of land along the North Branch of
the Raritan, once mined for iron, resisted the digging. But
you wanted a garden and I wanted you happy. So we dug
and heaved and split and threw into the river bed all the
unburied stones. You sank four stakes, expertly measured with
your artist eye, marked by string, a sacred ground. Seven years
that garden thrived in the shadow of the bamboo stand and
on midsummer nights, the fireflies in a synchronized pulse
illuminated snap peas, squash, cucumbers, carrots, tomatoes,
kohlrabi, lettuce, radish, green beans, peppers. We drank red
wine, listening to the music of the humming water, munching
snap peas, barefooted, with shoots of light darting through
the trees, a spider web spotlighted, kisses, a vespers of sorts on
consecrated land.

To Taste

Going down easy
With a chewed yet smooth surface

Calling up simple things
With a hint of memory

Resting on my tongue
A wafer
Of communion
Offered in peace

As we speak softly
To each other without words.

2

what I didn't know before

Tracings

In the pose of the reclining sea maiden,
the young girl lies frozen for hours
as the artist draws his power
across the sand—I pass this place
too many times to remember, looking
for her eyes—the girl, not the mermaid—
and I can't find them, somehow lost
in the sand sculpture, blinded
by the sun and moving bodies.

The sculptor's fingers draw life
lines, and the mermaid breathes
as light chisels through the space
between people walking along Commercial Street,
some pausing to marvel at the girl's beauty,
some at the art of the mermaid.

I fail to sleep that night,
tracing my fingers over my body,
weeping foolishly for her face,
trying to give myself a little bit of life.

Last Long Looks

Last long looks, lake fog in the Maine woods,

years later, another look, another woman,

as the snow squall dims her face,

and the car door closes. Yet loss crystallizes

in that space of one forever missing

and the other lost in passages, now found.

Night Pools

The anticipation of that first time:
first look, lingering, first touch,
drawing nearer to the moisture and
the sound of my own breath.

Paying attention has taken me lifetimes, too long.
But you lead me through the woods deliberately,
quietly guiding me deeper into the dark,
closer to the peepers and tree frogs,
vernal pool after vernal pool.

I hear you exhale and whisper what might be my name into the net.
The spotted salamander struggles, but only momentarily, settles
with a firm grip onto your thumb. I open my hands to you, and
a shiver ripples through me. I want that first moment
over and over again, knowing what I know now—
how to touch more lightly, slowly, sighing
holding you, tenderly,
gently, in awe.

Not a Flashy Thing

It came out fully formed,
no lightning bolt or earthmoving,
far from a flashy thing. More like
a late summer afternoon tossed
together with sweet grapes, figs,
Manchego cheese, and prosecco.
That's how I loved you. Open
windows and a breezy light
with any plans made to be
broken. So when your smile
fell on me in the midst of your
cutting and chopping, I understood
what I didn't know before.

Acushla

At five in the afternoon,
snow has slowed to a seductive pace,
teasing with its intermittent touch.
The space between each flake
is vast and crisp with caution.

At five in the afternoon,
the blue teapot whistles and steams,
rattling me into the cedar room
where you lie quilted in sleep.
I hold my hands around the mug
warming my palms and watch
the rise and fall of your chest.

By six in the evening,
the snow drops
in a frenetic freefall
filling the silence with white,
and as you rouse,
I dive fiercely as each flake
into the hollow of your soul,
begging to be burned.

"Red Leaves"

to Elizabeth Catlett

Your large, flowing hand
covers the page of the book
and the words seep into that strong hand
up into the sinews of your able arms
across shoulders that have known the world
into the beautiful neck
that your tilted head rests upon.

Your eyes look skyward
out into a burst of red leaves
as you translate those words
into your own voice and wisdom.

How is a book a window,
how is a book a mirror,
how will you paint for me
a new wonder?

Ask Again

You ask again this evening
at what price does anger steal
from everyday tenderness,

abandonment, flood passion with pain.
Resting my head on your belly
I listen, ignoring your plea to hurt you,

grant you punishment.
I speak in tongues down
stomach to clit, staying for longer

than hate can muster.
Now I know that anger is fear
inside out, the monster of genetics:

What if I become…? I take you in,
swallow you whole. In the morning
I show you again what freedom is.

Late at Night

Thinking if I don't say the words
to myself, a whisper in my head,
I won't feel that hunger in my gut,

that slow spin of emptiness
so I read the words of others
late into the night

as the owl hoots gently,
not intending to cast a memory
in the shadows of the pine

across my desk
to the card where you have scribbled
"I miss you" in an illegible scrawl

I could read
no matter how disguised
our loneliness might be.

Mapping

Watching you sleep, moved by the shape of your body,
I wonder about the scars, childhood mishaps
provoked by your endless curiosity, marks
dropped on the surface from chicken pox, faint
as if you have been mapped by drops of soft rain,
and the memorials of love scratches from beloved cats
leaving Hansel-and-Gretel patterns on your hands
that have traced my own scars like reading a book.

Have you felt the tracks of my living in such quiet spaces
when my chest rises and falls against your back
pressing those scars into your sleeping form,
wishing you awake, shaken by the turning of your body?
Pages of braille, mysterious to the unfamiliar fingers,
you translate me into all our languages.

how can I say that things are pictures

our hands reach for different things
how can I write words
how can you model clay
how can either of us reach beyond
the things we know
to build the towers higher
to return families to the right number
to put the ordinary back into the daily

my fingers press to pen
suspended in the space
above the empty paper

your fingers flying in the air
poised in kinetic contemplation
near the brownish mound

our hands tossed against distance
and anger and hate and gods
fumble for a connection

how can we touch
when the walls are crumbling
and the silence says too much

who are you rescuing
from the suffocating mud
who am I resurrecting
from the limits of my imagination

—9/11/01

3

geographies of lives

This Place I Love

The land stretches backward
bent by rush of ocean's hard touches
arches into soft curve
mixes salty sweet bay
with light of evening.

You fall gently into my arms
head tilted back into moon rays
swaying into and away from my body
sweet salt of your startling neck
engulfs me into this place I love.

On Your Fourth Birthday

Someone caught you unaware
in a photograph on your fourth birthday.
You gaze in profile away
to some place you fill with small loves.
You greedily hold a tiny bear,
protecting it fiercely in your busy hands.

I have captured you in this pose,
a hazy light attaching itself to your skin,
as you stand, naked, after love.
Sometimes I wonder where you go
but am satisfied that in some way
you have held me as tightly
as those things you loved as a child.

Shedd Aquarium, Chicago, 2003

provoked by Pierre Huyghe's *Zoodram 5 (after* Sleeping Muse *by Constantin Brancusi)*

no chronology here
we only have our bodies
seconds of puncture
a blink
you on the other side
looking at   through the tank
constructed space
hermit crabs   arrow crabs
your favorites
our landscape
living in-between
worlds   meanings   languages
enclosure of crustaceans   basalt
your floating head
Brancusi's *Sleeping Muse*
asymmetrical face on my pillow
stolen in the night
there is no story here
just repeated object
strange   beautiful creatures
walking through the Shedd
after disruption
you hold my hand   another room
avoiding narrative arc
leaning in
sometimes our eyes meet   mostly not
watching you watch the crabs
part installation   part intimacy
you dream of swimming with dolphins

blink
you naked in Provincetown moonlight
blink
you deconstructed drifts
in the pause   we interrogate
absorb   take each other in
minerals interacting   charged
open my eyes   scene changed
crabs rotate
light shifts
you a shooting star
kiss my cheek   lips wet
eyes shine
bright stars in our constellation
where to next

That's All

The birds chirp at hint of first light
ease me out of fitful sleep but
soon jolted by a gentle sweep
across my instep like you often did
in early stirring, rolling over
reminding me you were here
fingers glide up the bottom of my foot
slide between my toes, up my calf, thigh
ass, inside me, a full-throated song
before sleep again, Sunday morning

Fully awake now, I know
the dog shifted in her sleep
under covers at the foot of the bed
brushing her fur against my skin
while you sleep in South Williamsburg
with a new wife
as I sprawl on this queen bed
no wrestling over blankets or
tossing your leg off me or
resenting the slow breaths of your dreaming.

What I Will Leave You

(Intimations on Mortality)

in a storage unit
boxes of books
over a thousand
a soft oversized
red red couch
ink drawing
of B. B. King
the sculpted
unbronzed
head of Pilate
(after reading
Song of Solomon)
desert photographs
notebooks
marble unstitched
lined unlined
sketch pads
scribbled poems
thoughts quotes
definitions research
ashes of the dog
named after the poet
what is left you
Noli timere
do not
be afraid

Stolen Poem

We must break in order to become
blue, the color of bruises,
believing everything would turn out right.
In your hesitation I found my answer,
the last loved object of his attention,
the raven-like night that slips
easily from your hands.

Phrases and lines in this poem are borrowed from Haruki Murakami,
Mark Doty, Lynda Hull, and Marie Howe.

Amor Mundi

No one can be blamed for loving
the fluffy puppy with chocolate eyes
floppy ears and feathery flapping tail
the golden one that catches a frisbee midair
retrieve to the thrower without command.

The dark mutt in the corner
shaggy hair masking frightened eyes
shakes whenever anyone gets too close
sighing whimpers as I bend down to cup her face.

She's the one I always bring home.

Mourning Flowers

For JMR (1971–2020)

I.

Marie wrote about what the living do   i answer by holding
my place in books that might save me   poems of the
geographies of lives i've lived   buried in the geology of my
body   like that bookmark Simon cherished   like callas when
he was dying   the one he got at Giovanni's Room before any
of us knew about   the fever & dying so many would do

II.

now today   word you died   cara   always almost loving
me   holding fast   laughing hard   a notion of what letting
go might yield   the volta in our poem   all style and rhythm
defying form   once familiar land

this death falls hard in basalt of ink on skin   the Triple
Morrigan we shared   eruption from the volcano   smoldering
for years from deadly yearning

III.

yellow ray flowers

corolla and ovaries

dark center of disks

phyllaries a tender hand

fields of eternal lightness

IV.

at the end   i would read *The Book of Tea* like you tended your
garden   (squash   corn   beans)   in the middle of night
headlamp on   to stop the torrent of nightmare   i read pages
i tagged years before   Okakura reminding us   a butterfly is a
flower with wings

Memory Chain

Eating my words whole
the letters come back at me
rearranged and angry

Spare light splices between
the pages of my notebook poems
once contained in an us

The migration of birds
tattoo the sky with patterns signifying
the promise to return

Rearranged and angry
in empty rooms splashed with colors
I reimagine a life

The pages of my notebook
poems of love transformed by shadows
resurrected as palimpsest

My words in your mouth
whisper the rhythms of soaring
a migration of birds

Moments of clarity
like hair raised on the back of the neck
warn of predators.

A Controlled Burn

I.

That tree always knows
when a storm lurks.
She sways lightly,
turns her leaf hands

skyward, open,
waiting for the rain,
ready to adjust to a hardness
or a softness.
The storm feeds her,
makes her brighter from the inside out.

Not all storms destroy.
Most rearrange the landscape
in a way imperceptible to the eye,
but the tree knows, adjusts,
and becomes steadier.

II.

You touched my cheek
with a lightness that cracked
me open, raw,
a strike of lightning
that set me on fire
and saved me,
a necessary burning,
creating soil for a new planting.

4

recipe for daydreams

Torch Song

The evening lightning flashed across the skies
throughout the late spring dinner party.
When only a rumble was left, your eyes
softened in the porch light, clarity,
a reckoning to kiss you, declare love,
or not to choose living, or despair.
So when the call comes as thunder roars above,

four this morning, Bill dead, too young, unfair,
I dive into thoughts of you, dear,
struggle to force words to rip and roar, chasing chaos,
frantically grabbing for images out of fear
that if I can't create then I will fall into loss.

You touch my face in the sunrising light on the porch,
another storm over, a morning bright, your eyes, my torch.

Burnt

There are escapes and true things

in this recipe for daydreams

improvised so long ago

—a dash of motorcycle on open road

outside Galisteo, no helmets, hair

blows around our faces in wild gyrations,

your arms around my waist in afternoon haze

—a pinch of New Orleans in July heat,

a dark club underground lit by jazz

saxophone, your skin glistens in sweat

as we lean close over bourbon straight

—a smidgeon of Tiburon, hands held

at twilight, a hint of weed from hours

ago mixes with the scent of the bay air

—salt and pepper to taste in a tent in Arcadia

where leaving me was not

an option, your tongue in my mouth,

all the words I ever need.

Deep Grooves

after Gwendolyn Brooks and Tom Waits

Will she remember my voice
while I fight the tears?

Abortion never lets you forget.
Or forgive. Ex-boyfriend she fucked
when I was too busy to answer her calls.
My drive with her to the clinic
then rocking her to sleep for nights
as we wept for the child I promised to raise.

Will she remember my voice
while I fight the tears?

She swore she was straight but
loved me hard with desperate insistence.
My anger burnt a hole between us.
Her guilt froze it over. Cold night
nightmares of her bent over the toilet,
sobbing over raging clots of blood propels me
to search her name. I write a love letter,
ask no reply, request unwritten remembrance.

Will she remember my voice
while I fight the tears?

The album spins in amber light,
songs gather our dust
in deep, fine-tuned grooves,
what vibrated between us still
bounces inside this solitary lover.
How old would our child be?

Blue Morning

Come blue morning off the foothills
    before the sun rises above earth

           new moon of blackest summer

      the faint song of a Northern flicker
    a prelude to its calling and drumming

as you sleep beside me on this ground
heavy head on my pins-and-needles arm

    I am reluctant to move you and such sweetness

      knowing morning blue changes as do all seasons

         fragile as the bird's wing,

   even in flight.

Iterations

What's in a name but
spaces filled with others' notions
of who I am to them inhabited
by the performance of love, or not,
name left for another name
but staying to haunt, a ghost
of tender moments and tense encounters,
a tattoo of the person I am always becoming.

Martin Jude in my prebirth form, red-haired
giant of an Irish grandfather plus
the patron saint of hopeless cases,
rewritten by my mother's disappointment
in a girl baptized Kathleen Ann
for both grandmothers cursed with early death,
with a sexy Margaret added by the Archbishop
in Sacred Heart Cathedral at my confirmation
where I crushed all the questions
with answers backed by heresy and sass.
High school of Kathleens, Ellens, Marys,
and Marias christened with last names
to avoid the confusion of teen identities
while stoking our revolt against the patriarchy.
Nicknames from teaching and coaching,
shortened versions, initials, and my favorite,
Dr. K, not because of the Dr., but for the reminder
of my favorite basketball player, Julius Erving,
Dr. J, although I played in suede blue Clydes.

As if there again, transported, these hours of snow
soothe me back to the cold apartment over the deli
where you kissed me for the first time. I opened

my eyes to the moon littered with flakes,
your breath on my neck whispering "Kath."

That home has long vanished despite the specter
of you in every touch and soft look.
I live now with bodies of other women
in gentle boxes floating on a screen
creating new habitats to inhabit.
I am Kat; poems are my sanctuary.

A Canyon in My Throat

In my chest, there is a hole

as wide as the canyon in my throat.

Climb through windows of ribs and see

a river flowing, red and blue sparkles,

igniting a fire blazing in the swell of heart and lungs,

unvirginal devotion to the Blessed Mary.

Put your ear to belly and hear

a jangle of bracelets, wind chimes catching

the words of breeze, sending an alphabet of gurgles

into intricate weavings of veins.

Press mouth to palm and taste

a finch feeding your lifeline, sustaining our young.

For Sweetness

Succulent red apples

sliced open

yield a crisp,

sweating meat,

mixed with the dried juice

of the apricot

trapped on your fingertips

and under your nails,

brushing my face

in a gesture of seduction

and you turn to dip two fingers

in honey,

passionate as a worker bee,

bring those fingers

to my lips,

where I almost drown.

Blowing Glass

Somewhere in this body rests a murrine
of who you were to me
one last night.

Forged in fire and rapid turning,
a shape filled with your breath,
we were always on the verge

of a drop and a shattering,
broken to a fineness beyond repair.
So when the perfect failure

never happened, our incalmo remaining
whole yet imperfect,
we embraced the heat

of one final moment
rather than settle
for an annealed life.

Blue Fields

Let me begin again
As pitch pine loved
By wind of intense tones
Gently stroked by breeze
Blown sideways in blizzard
Our intimacy accompanied
By birdsong as I whisper
Deeply from long needles
Cry out from the shortest
A frenzy of sounds carved
Out of such still silence
Let me begin again
Walk blue fields with you

Acknowledgments

My gratitude to the journals, magazines, and anthologies that published the following poems in this book, some in earlier versions:

Digging Through the Fat: "Iterations"
Divine Feminist: An Anthology of Poetry & Art by Womxn & Non-Binary Folx (2021): "Diversity of Matter"
Lavender Review: "Mapping"
Limp Wrist Magazine: "A Canyon in My Throat"
Moving Words Project/ARTS By the People (2020): "The Curve of Things" (short version/film)
The Night Heron Barks: "Mourning Flowers"
Platform Review: "Blue Fields" and "Shedd Aquarium, Chicago, 2003"
Sensations Magazine: "Blowing Glass"
Soup Can Magazine: "Not a Flashy Thing"
Stay Salty: Life in the Garden State, Vol. 2 (2021): "A Vespers of Sorts" and "Wild West"
Stillwater Review: "The Curve of Things" (long version)
Writing the Land: Northeast Anthology (2021): "Night Pools"

Gratitudes

For the enthusiastic and motivating early support of the title poem from Marina Carreira, David Crews, Nick Davis, Jean LeBlanc, and Dimitri Reyes that has never wavered. They have been champions for this book in uncountable ways.

For those readers of the manuscript over the years (many named in other gratitudes), especially Tamara Zbrizher, whose astute and incisive reading and organizational suggestions late in the process transformed *The Curve of Things* into the book you hold in your hands.

For the CavanKerry Press team: Gabriel Cleveland for his attention, patience, and wisdom throughout production; Baron Wormser for his kindness and generosity, making the final edits a poetic exchange that provided me with a lesson in grace; and Joy Arbor for her copyediting prowess, a skill I value more than she knows.

For my poetry family who sustains and inspires my creative life: Rachelle Parker, Donyah Richardson-Thurmond, Ras Heru Stewart, Paul Rabinowitz, Shane Wagner, and my Write On! Poetry Babes (not named in other gratitudes): Lynne McEniry, paulA neves, Dr. Grisel Y. Acosta, and Claudia Cortese.

For Ysabel Y. Gonzalez, who wrote a generous and tender foreword. I am humbled. Her commitment to encouraging my work and fostering poetry in the larger community is unflagging and noteworthy.

For Attorious René Augustin, Marina Carreira, and Darla Himeles, whose poetic and intelligent blurbs are beacons for the book and sirens for the urgent call of poetry in our times.

For Sarah Klein, who graciously shared her gorgeous artwork for the cover of my dreams.

For Amy Inglis and her ability to capture heart and spirit in my author photo.

For the people who have loved me, housed me, fed me, listened to me, and supported my dreams during the living and writing of this book: Kristen Ames, Sarah Anderson, Duncan Clegg, Brenda Derogatis, Nancy Ellis, Michele Fagan, Doug Farrand, Sheila Kelleher, Kathy Kremins (the Original), Marianne Lloyd, Meredith Martin, Melissa McHugh, Sean McHugh, Dorri Ramati, Alexander Rosenberg, Bethany Shenise, Jean Vitrano, Jane Waddell, and Melissa Woerner.

For my teachers whose poems I have read until the pages frayed and whose voices and lessons vibrate throughout this book: Ellen Bass, Cheryl Clarke, Carol Ann Duffy, June Jordan, Audre Lorde, Mary Oliver, and Adrienne Rich.

For Kiera McHugh, Cate McHugh, Arlo Clegg, and Felix Clegg. I write for you.

CavanKerry's Mission

A not-for-profit literary press serving art and community, CavanKerry is committed to expanding the reach of poetry and other fine literature to a general readership by publishing works that explore the emotional and psychological landscapes of everyday life, and to bringing that art to the underserved where they live, work, and receive services.

Other Books in the
Florenz Eisman Memorial Series

This book was printed on paper from responsible sources.

The Curve of Things was typeset in Bely, a classy throwback text font family built upon classical proportions to capitalize on reading familiarity. It was created by Roxane Gataud for TypeTogether in 2016.